EASY-TO-DRAW

ANIMALS

by Brenda Sexton & Jannie Ho

PICTURE WINDOW BOOKS

a capstone imprint

MATERIALS

Before you start your amazing drawings, there are a few things you'll need.

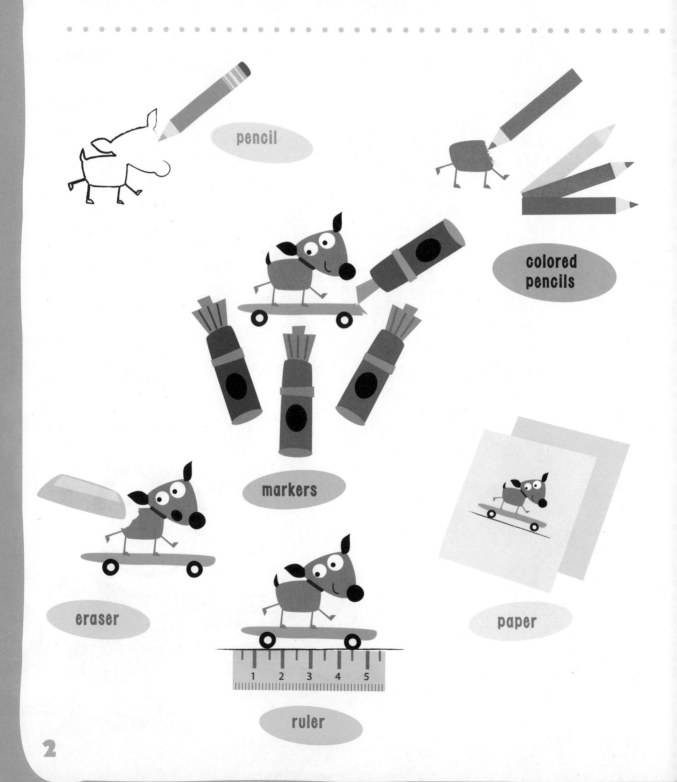

pencil

colored pencils

markers

eraser

paper

ruler

SHAPES

Drawing can be easy! If you can draw these simple letters, numbers, and shapes, YOU CAN DRAW anything in this book.

letters

A B C D
T U W

numbers

1 2 3

shapes

lines

Turtleneck

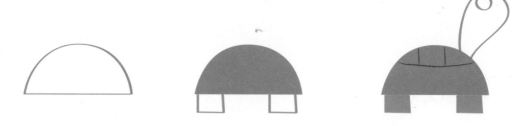

Potbellied Pig

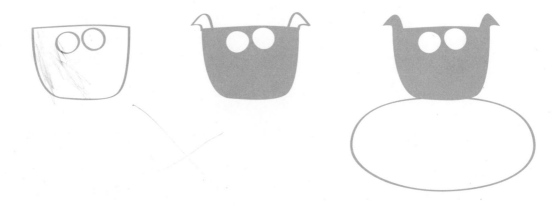

Crazy Quacker

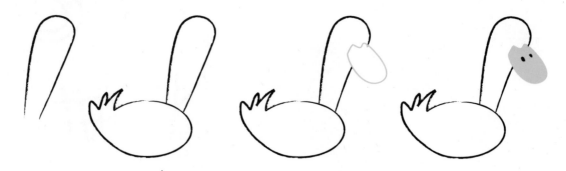

4

Now try this!

Oink! Oink!

Quack! Quack!

Quack!

Quack!

Polar Bear

Parrot

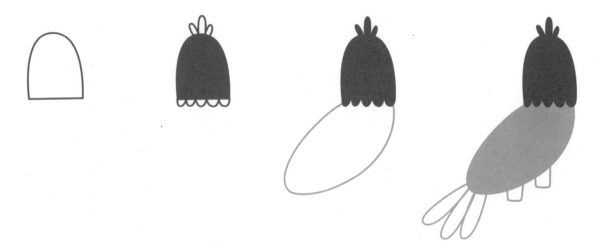

Snake

Bunny Hop

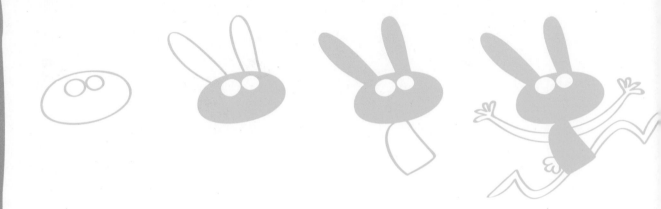

Super Mouse

Polka-Dotted Snake

Zebra

Elephant

Ostrich

Electric Cat!

Smart Kitten

Furry Feline

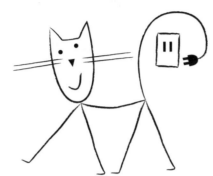

13

Penguin

Crocodile

Kangaroo

Tortoise

Giddyap Pony

Seeing Dog

Lion

Tiger

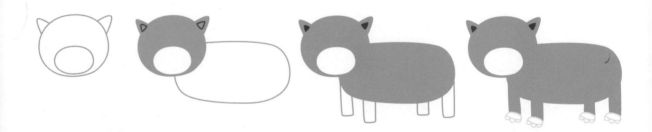

Monkey

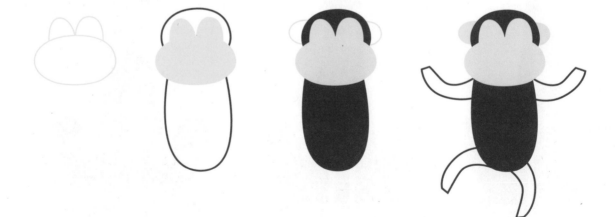

Hungry Froggie

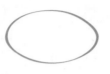   

Dancing Spider

Little Lizard

Hamster Race

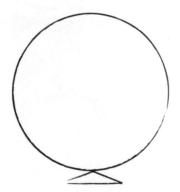 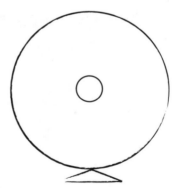 

20

Yum! Yum!

  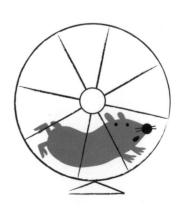

21

Dog Gone It!

Bye, Bye, Birdie!

  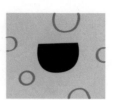 

Fish Dinner

Silly Kitty

Chirp! Chirp!

Now try this! →

23

Whale

Hippo

Shark

Giraffe

Anteater

Seal

Paw Prints

Hungry Pup

Skater Dog

Shaggy Pooch

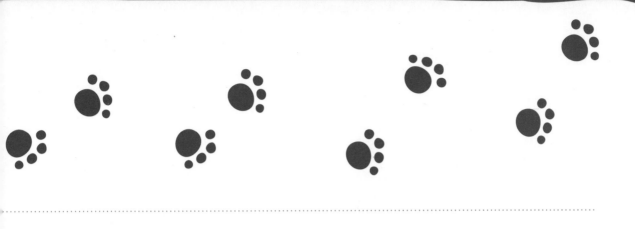

ARF!

29

Llama

Panda

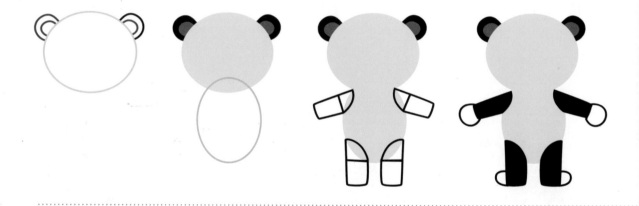

Prairie Dog

Flashy Fish

Fish Tank

Cool Catfish

Hermit Crab Catcher

Koala

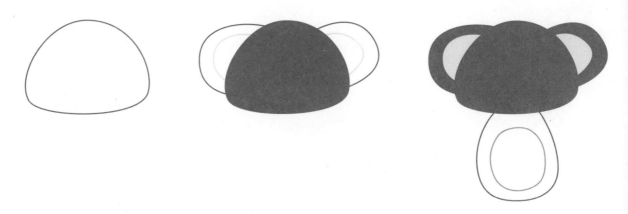

Chick

Porcupine

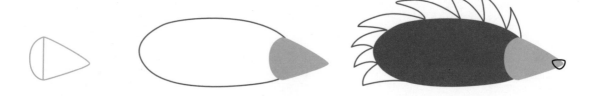

Now that you've drawn all the fuzzy and furry animals, round them up and

36

add some crazy props.

What do you get?

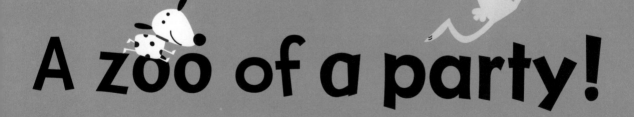

A zoo of a party!

Have fun creating
your masterpiece!

Teeter-Totter

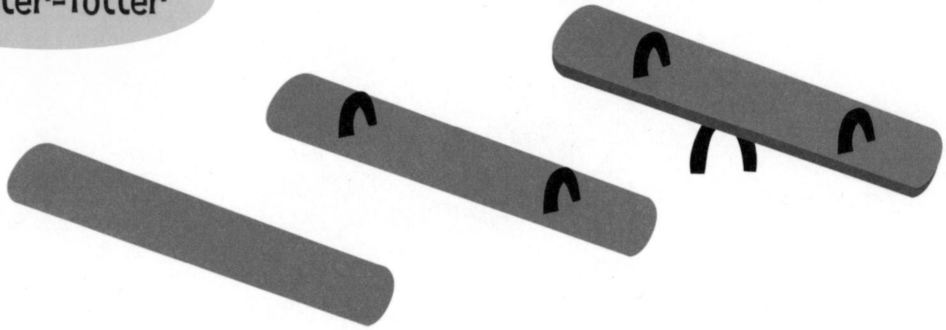

Trash Can

Swing Set

Skyline

Slide

Park Bench

Fountain

39

41

Bamboo

Rocks

Sun

Diving Board

Beach Ball

Tree

Waves

Grass

Clouds

Palm Tree

Flowers

Shrub

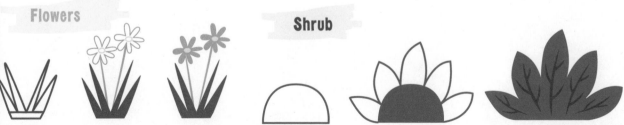

43

About the Authors

Brenda Sexton wishes she could live inside the colorful illustration world she creates. She has been honored for her whimsical illustrations by the Society of Children's Book Writers and Illustrators. She has also won four Emmy Awards for her work in sports television. Brenda lives and finds inspiration in the sunny California beach town of Marina Del Rey. Visit her at brendasexton.com.

Jannie Ho is also known as "Chicken Girl." Born in Hong Kong and raised in Philadelphia, Jannie studied at Parsons The New School for Design in New York City, earning a BFA in illustration. After working as a graphic designer and an art director at places such as Nickelodeon, Scholastic, and *Time Magazine for Kids*, she decided that illustration was her true calling. Jannie now specializes in illustrating for the children's market, with her work appearing in both trade and educational books, magazines, toys, crafts, and digital media. Visit her at www.chickengirldesign.com.

Picture Window Books
151 Good Counsel Drive
P.O. Box 669
Mankato, MN 56002-0669
877-845-8392
www.capstonepub.com

Editor: Shelly Lyons
Designer: Matt Bruning and Tracy Davies
Art Director: Nathan Gassman
Production Specialist: Sarah Bennett
The illustrations in this book were created digitally.

Library of Congress Cataloging-in-Publication Data
Cataloging-in-publication information is on file with the Library of Congress.
ISBN 978-1-4048-6760-4

Printed in Shenzhen, Guangdong, China.
112010
006015